Write Anyway!
Creative Writing Prompts, Journal Ideas & Essays that Crush Writer's Block!

by
David Bain

David Bain

*...with thanks to all my
writing teachers*

Table of Contents

*Each essay is followed by journal exercises and
story prompts*

David Bain

Your Infinite Playground

I.

If you're a writer and you don't keep a journal, I'm not going to say you should.

(But you should.)

Unless you're a surrealist or Dadaist, your work in progress is going to be somewhat fettered. The very nature of work meant for others to read - everything from a shopping list to an epic novel - is that it generally has to be linear or otherwise constrained in terms of topic, in terms of scope, in terms of grammar and punctuation, etc.

A journal is none of these things.

When I ask students early in the semester of an entry level writing class to keep a journal, most of them invariably groan. Most of them envision bleeding heart "dear diary" entries written by fourteen-year-old girls on the verge of suicide because their favorite member of their favorite boy band hasn't followed them yet on Twitter.

That or they imagine it's to be filled with entries about trees and flowers and birds.

A journal can certainly be all that.

But, God, I hope yours isn't.

***

Your journal is *utterly you.*

A space of your own that no one else sees, where you can do and say whatever the hell you want, with no spell- or grammar-check.

It's almost scary, all that white space when you pick up a blank journal.

But think again: Having a place where you are beholden to no one and nothing can be utterly liberating.

Notice I said *place.* Yes, a writer's

journal is a sort of gym for all sorts of potential mental exercise, but it's also a physical thing.

***

Before I explain what I mean by that, I want to add that I highly suggest a physical journal. One you can write in longhand.

Online journals and blogs are meant for public consumption and they're an entirely different sort of writing than I'm talking about here.

Same goes with a typed journal. You're more likely to worry the writing, to autocorrect and edit. You're more likely to fret about structure and content - with a pen and paper, there is no backspace.

A flimsy spiral bound pad from the Dollar General works just as well as a sleek Moleskine notebook. In fact, I suggest the cheaper, the better - you won't feel as "precious" about what goes into it.

***

Journals are why I do not believe in writer's block.

How can you have writer's block when you can write down any words whatsoever that might be in your head? It's perhaps the ultimate irony that you could easily fill a journal with words about how you can't write.

No one will judge your journal. No one will review your journal. You can burn it after you write it in it!

(Though I hope you don't!)

***

Your journal doesn't have to be all words, if you don't want it to be. There's the whole scrapbooking phenomenon for one thing, but for me that's too formal - too much a construction meant to be viewed by others - too arranged, too *appropriate*. Your journal could easily consist of drawings - even if you can't draw at all. It can consist of newspaper clippings, gluesticked collages, pressed four-leaf clovers, etc., etc., etc.

***

When you think of a writer's journal, it pays to think of it as a physical space. Your journal is an office desk, good for taking notes, getting rote tasks finished, fleshing out plans for the work in progress, outlining to do lists, hanging motivational posts to keep yourself on task, and generally getting yourself organized.

But your journal is also a vacation, your personal writer's retreat. It's a cozy, hidden mountain cabin or a sprawling skyscraper of a Caribbean hotel, both with a perfect view. All your favorite contemporary writers as well as all the greatest writers of history are staying there, waiting at your beck and call. Just write down your questions and you'll often find your own pen answering.

Your journal is the cheapest psychiatric office you'll ever find. Sit behind your desk and listen as you lie on the couch and chatter away. The session doesn't need to end after an hour; you won't be charged extra for running over. And your journal doesn't mind if you call after midnight.

Your journal is a warehouse, its aisles stretching off far as the eye can see, the shelves filled with every writing tool you will ever need. You'll have to work hard to get to some - you'll have to walk more miles than it might seem worth, but you'll get there. You'll have to stretch to reach others. You might have to even jump - you'll only gain possession of some particular writing tools in this warehouse after numerous repeat attempts to access them.

Your journal is a playground. There doesn't appear to be an end to the fun and games. Don't you dare sulk in the corner! There are skip-ropes for routine workouts. There are jungle gyms for when you're feeling a little more daring. There are wide-open spaces for the playing-out of epic battles. There are benches for when you're feeling quiet and contemplative. There are endless sandboxes and blocks where you can build whatever you might imagine. There are virgin   jungles to explore. And over here, lined up and waiting, is every sort of playmate imaginable - but there aren't any bullies, unless you want one around. The playhouses! Check *them* out! Why, they're made of whatever substance you like: plain wood, candy, alien adamantite, glowing green jade, soft pillows, rain. They are huts. They are mansions. They are home and spa, museum and studio all in one.

And over there, at the edge of the page, there at the spot where you flip over to the next page, there's a beach with a ship about to set sail to whatever country, whatever world, whatever emotion, whatever future or past, whatever memory - real or false, true or imagined - whatever dream, whatever universe, whatever facet of *you* you might like.

Journal Prompts

1. Describe your journal as a place. Repeat this exercise from time to time. There is no reason for this place to remain consistent or static, unless you want it to!

2. Describe, in great detail, the perfect writing place and circumstances for you. This might be significantly different from #1. Try to include every sense, the weather, the time of day, etc. Again, this is a repeatable, changeable exercise.

3. Brainstorm a long list of things you might be able to journal about. Preferably this is a list of things you have never yet journaled about. Refer to (and possibly expand) this list anytime you don't feel inspired, don't feel like writing, etc.

4. Describe, in great detail, your perfect mansion. This is an imaginative exercise, so it's fine if

you want, for instance, the Caribbean coast outside the west wing and the Mediterranean outside the east. There is no square foot limit, nor are you bound by any sort of physics - unless you want to be!

5. Find a physical object worthy of being taped or glued into your journal. Write at least a page about why you've chosen to save this item.

6. Write a meditation on the different types of journaling - notebook journaling, typed journaling, Facebook, blogging, etc. - and what each might mean for you.

Story Prompts

1. Write a story about someone who manages to enter an imaginative realm they've created. You could go anywhere from there. Perhaps it's the only place they can be with a certain lover. Perhaps the place comes under attack from…? Perhaps this haven changes against their will. Etc.

2. Write a story about a hotel where the guest list is impossible. What sort of conversations and intrigues might take place?

3. Write a story from the point of view of the journal of an alien or fantasy character. Perhaps a time traveler visiting our era.

4. Take an old journal (if you have one) or your current one and open to a random, already filled page. Point to a random spot on that page. Write a story stemming from the word or sentence or

whatever else you might find there. Repeat at will.

5. Write a story about people living in a house made of an unusual substance or materials. While this could indeed be a fantasy tale, it certainly doesn't have to be!

6. Lots of fiction takes the form of a protagonist's journal entries. What's something you haven't seen done with this form yet? Remember that anything goes in journals! *Go there!* Then take it to the next level!

The Muse Doesn't Live
in Your Window

Former U.S. Poet Laureate W. S. Merwin writes that his mentor John Berryman once suggested he literally get down on his knees and pray to The Muse, and I agree that's probably a good thing for a mentor to say to a new writer.

In order to *want to write,* you must, at some point in your life, see the written word as sacred. You need to be in thrall to the very act, the very concept of writing. You need to have beatific visions of immaculately constructed novels. You need to allow the revelation of a perfectly placed comma, the divine choosing of an articulately exact word to send you into ecstatic awe. And you need to believe, early on, that The Muse is responsible. You need to believe she will carry and protect you and envelop you in Her golden glow when the evil demon Writer's Block insinuates His way into your life. You need to believe the words pouring forth from your fingertips are inspired from The Great Beyond or, sitting there, typing away in your cold, bare, lonely garret or dorm room, you will lose all hope.

But then, to get to the next stage, you need eventually to lose your religion.

Not your passion, not your awe, and certainly not your craft, but you need to stop worshipping The Muse.

And simply trust her.

To have a long-term career in writing, your Muse needs to become your friend, your constant companion, not your Goddess.

Your office is not your church, and your laptop is not an altar.

Starbucks is not a holy place, and your journal, your short story, your novel is not a Bible.

Your words might eventually move readers spiritually. But your tools are mundane and secular. They are the same words available to every other person using your language.

More plainly put: The first, most important thing you can do to avoid writer's block is to stop seeing your writing as sacred.

The ultimate truth about The Muse is this: She is not there to provide you with inspiration or story ideas or poetic turns of phrase. That's not her job. Those things are *your* job.

The Muse is more like a nurse in an operating room, while you're the surgeon. She is there to hand you the tools you already know how to use. In fact, she's usually utterly silent, just letting you work. But she also knows the surgeon, the artist, better than he knows himself. So sometimes she might suggest a different tool, a different instrument, a different procedure, but she'd never do the surgery herself.

The point is there is fervent, important, painstaking work being done in this operating room, and The Muse is there to facilitate it. All the passions that long ago prompted the surgeon to go into this line of work are there in that room. The nurse, The Muse, is simply a quiet, trusted, calming presence, allowing the artist to focus and perform what might appear, to some looking on from the outside, to be miracles.

Let me tell you the story of when I learned to stop worshipping The Muse and, instead, let her be my coach, kicking my butt into writing gear.

When I was in my twenties I lived

in a little cabin on a small lake. A big picture window took up most of the wall in the back room. It looked out over the small deck and down a long, green slope to the dock where I kept my rowboat. From there the view offered an incredible vista of the sprawling woods and secluded homes on the other side of the sparkling waters. That view was what sold me on the cabin on my initial tour of the place.

Ah!, I thought, gazing at the scene spread out before me. *Inspiration! The perfect place to write!* I set up my scribe's station at the foot of that window before I'd ever unpacked anything else. The station, for the time I lived in that cozy little place, consisted of an old folding chair, a wobbly card table and a word processor as big and bulky as, say, your modern-day countertop convection oven.

But guess what.

The Muse didn't live in that view outside the window.

The scene beyond my writing station remained beautiful, to be sure. In the summer I'd see endless small boats gliding on the lake. I could watch a single fisherman's progress from his arrival at dawn until his exodus at dusk. In winter I would watch families playing on the ice, skating, practicing hockey, dogs skidding and sliding across the slick surface. I would sit there for hours, watching the sailboats, watching the trees swaying in the breeze, watching the girls sun themselves, watching the cookouts, the clouds, the family of raccoons that set up camp near the cabin.

Yes, all quite quaint and pretty.

But I didn't write much.

Finally, up against a deadline one afternoon, fed up with my lack of progress, I clumsily hefted the boxy word processor into my arms and stalked off into the kitchen, lugging my writing station to the corner, facing the wall, no window within my field of sight, just boring faux wood paneling.

The Muse approved. I finished my project and, for the remainder of the time I lived in that little house, more than doubled my output.

And I still write this way, when I have a choice. My current office has nice skylight windows looking out over miles of Indiana backroads and hills. But I write with my back to them.

That afternoon, when I schlepped the word processor into the kitchen, was the day I stopped seeing writing as a church requiring a cathedral.

The kitchen is, in fact, nearly the perfect metaphor. Work and skill and, yes, creativity - for creativity certainly is required in a decent kitchen - are all sparks for bringing that element we call The Muse into our lives. The kitchen is a place requiring toil and constant care, but it's also a place of warmth and joy and continued sustenance. If we have the right tools and techniques in our kitchen, if we learn to skillfully mix and play with and adapt the tools and utensils and recipes and ingredients at hand, there is literally no end to the fires we can spark and the possibilities we can cook up!

The Muse is simply *there*, waiting, an element, literally all around.

Sometimes we have no control over the elements - fire, water, earth and air, all of them can come roaring into our lives, taking over and leaving us helpless in their wake. Same with The Muse. Sometimes she simply drops a story in your lap, fully formed. And those days are wonderful.

But usually, to take advantage of an element, we have to strike the match or turn on the tap ourselves. The Muse is the fire inherent in a piece of wood. She's just waiting for your spark to ignite the flame.

Journal Prompts

1. What is your relationship with The Muse?

2. Where do you write? Why there?

3. Imagine your Muse as a person and describe them in detail.

4. Why do writers get annoyed when asked why they write?

5. Do you have any superstitions about your craft? Why or why not? If so, what are they?

6. Write a "recipe" for creativity.

Story Prompts

1. Write a story about a writer or artist who literally meets their Muse.

2. Write a story about an artist who is lacking inspiration. What caused their slump? Do they get back on track? If so, how? Does their work change significantly?

3. Write a story which draws a parallel between some sort of physical work and beauty or art.

4. Write a story in which one of the elements (earth, air, fire, water) becomes a metaphor for beauty or art.

5. Write a story about the relationship between a surgeon and a nurse - or any other type of "professional" and his/her "helper".

6. Write a story about someone who receives all sorts of accolades, perhaps even riches and awards, without putting in any effort or work. Why do they get this award? What are the responses?

David Bain

What the Hell Is This Thing Doing in My Story?

So you suddenly find your characters are just sort of standing around in the middle of your book, waiting for what's next. You're not ready for a big antagonist attack yet. A new character would be too huge an undertaking at this point. But you need a bridge to the next Major Plot Point. And you're all dialogued out.

Out of nowhere, it seems: Momentum zero.

This point in the fictional piece can certainly feel like writer's block.

But it's really a new element of your story waiting to be born.

You'll run into these situations whether you're strictly a seat-of-your-pants type of writer or you write according to a fifty-page outline you painstakingly crafted before you ever wrote actual word one of your novel. Unexpected moments are the nature of good fiction - unexpected for the reader as well as the writer.

And the solution to the these sudden horse latitudes in the sea of your work in progress is often just as unexpected - just like a ship that's caught in the doldrums can suddenly set sail on a wind out of nowhere, the unexpected can add new life to your story.

One of my favorite tricks to jump-start my writing in a scene suddenly grown stagnant is to introduce an unexpected object. Unexpected by not only the characters, but by me as well.

I'll make a mental list of three or four completely random objects. And I do find it best if they are *objects*, concrete items that can be handled, examined, experienced by the senses. I try to avoid things around me in my office or wherever I happen to be writing. I might even do this with my eyes closed. One method I use is to imagine the globe of the earth, seen from afar, with a sudden zoom-in on a random spot. What object do you find there? Add it to the list.

A feather, a wrench, a stray piece of linoleum tile.

A computer chip, a Mason jar, a little stick man.

That's my list for now. Does one "feel" more right than the other? That's the one I go with.

The unexpected object can give your characters something to discuss, to touch, to wonder about, to tell a story about.

Sometimes this object will just give you the little push you needed to get you through the scene.

Other times it might well transform the entire story.

In my crime/horror novel *Gray Lake*, there's a scene fairly early on when the characters are in a car, talking about everything I need them to talk about. And as I was writing, I realized there is, as Jerry Lee Lewis might put it, *a whole lotta talkin' goin' on.* Not quite infodump levels of talk, but getting there. I needed something to break it up, to enliven the scene and add a sense of wonder or at least curiosity to it instead of just more rote this-needs-to-be-said, plotty-plot-plot dialogue.

The car they are in is a beater just purchased "as is" from a junkyard by one of the protags. There's a box of old CDs, cassettes (yes, cassettes) and other old detritus in the back seat. Perfect place for an unexpected object. I don't remember what other objects might have been on my list, but in this case, what my subconscious came up with was fairly unimpressive - a set of keys on a fob. Except, *hm*, a more conscious part of my brain mused, what if these keys didn't fit the car? And what if the shape of the fob held a slightly ominous portent?

I won't spoil the story by telling you more, but the keys and fob served their purpose. They broke up the relative monotony of the dialogue - not that my dialogue is ever monotonous, he said, keeping his audience riveted - and gave the characters and the reader something to wonder about.

It also gave me, the writer, something to wonder about.

Again, no spoilers, but suffice it to say the fob is quickly forgotten by the characters, but plays an interesting symbolic part toward the end of the novel when it surfaces again.

Usually, if you hit this static point in a scene or in your book and you come up with a list of unexpected objects, one will not just "feel" right, as I suggested above, one will all but *scream* to be included. It's like the needy yowl of a cat wanting to be let in. In my experience it's best to listen to this insistent beastie, even though you might spend a few minutes - or maybe even a day or two - wondering *What the hell is this thing doing in my story?*

Don't worry. You'll find that this object, risen up out of nowhere, eventually fits.

Why is this?

Well, Michael Jackson said he often felt, while writing his songs, that he was unearthing something that was already there - that he was just a conduit, revealing music that was simply sitting around, waiting for him to discover it. Stephen King has made similar comments about writing fiction.

I'm not going to come straight out and say writing is a mystic act, digging into the already extant archives of Jung's collective unconscious. I'm not necessarily saying your unexpected object was plucked out of the ether by fate because it was cosmically *supposed* to be in your story. Just as likely your unexpected item really is totally random, but you've told yourself the object is important and your subconscious takes over and fits it into the story, sometimes quite quickly.

Take whichever explanation you're more comfortable with.

But either way, the thrill of the unexpected is why we read fiction. Even in the most by-rote, heavily outlined and plotted, give-the-people-what-they-want, pumped-out-for-the-money, genre-of-the-month novel, there's the distant spark of *something new in the world.*

I'll put forth this thrill of the unexpected is why we *write* fiction as well. As writers, we have not only the freedom, but the *duty* to surprise our readers - and ourselves as well.

Journal Prompts

1. Make a long, random list of surprise objects to insert in stories

2. Write about how a real-life unexpected object once changed your life - or maybe just your day.

3. What have your favorite surprises been in books you've read, in movies you've watched, and in real life?

4. What is the relationship between writing and the subconscious?

5. Write about a real-life time you were "stuck in the doldrums". How did you get out of it?

6. Write about dreams you might have had involving unusual or unexpected objects.

Story Prompts

1. Your character has spent their entire life inside a building, not knowing there's a whole world outside. One day, they find a door and open it. What do they see?

2. Your protagonist wakes one day to find something unusual in the middle of the kitchen floor that definitely wasn't there the night before. What is it? How did it get there? What happens next?

3. Your protagonist sees a madman running down the city street raving about a seemingly commonplace object they are waving above their heads. Fill in the backstory and what happens next.

4. While digging for change, your character finds something in the couch cushions that changes their life forever…

5. Write a story about the most

unusual (or perhaps mundane) object you can think of for a murder weapon.

6. Aliens come to earth and request a certain common object from every household. Why?

David Bain

Write Anyway

I.

The problem is the current story sucks.

The problem is another book in the series just got a one-star review on Amazon.

The problem is my entire catalog sucks.

The problem is I suck.

I should be in a different business - and I am. I teach plus I have a day job. Can't make it by writing alone. So why do I bother? I should give up the early morning scribbling, just teach, become one of those English profs who teaches the stuff but doesn't really write much. Maybe have a buddy who's an editor publish something from time to time so I can keep tenure - I mean who really reads that academic stuff anyway?

I'm probably not qualified to teach, either, not really, so I should just keep slogging away with the day job, chasing that legal tender, go home at night and watch TV, get an extra hour of sleep in the morning.

It's not fair that I've been at this for twenty years and that guy on that writing podcast had overnight success by gaming the system.

It's not fair that I look at the awards on the wall, the good reviews, the newsletter list of fans, all my books on the shelf and it means nothing. Evidence of a life wasted.

What bugs me is the last book didn't have quite the launch I anticipated.

What bugs me is that I did everything the blogging guru suggested and nothing happened.

What bugs me is no one has signed up for my newsletter in days.

What bugs me is every piece, in the end, is so much different than my original vision. The result, after all that labor and toil, is invariably a bruised, beaten, bloodied, monstrous *lusus naturea.*

The problem is Author X does it all so much better than I do.

The problem is Author Y sucks and her sales are sky high while mine aren't.

The problem is Author Z, to whom I can only hope to aspire, is a genius and is starving.

The problem is the world won't listen.

II.

I'm writing this piece because I'm procrastinating on another.

III.

Write anyway.

Even if the piece sucks.

Write anyway, even if you know *you* suck.

Because you probably don't.

Probably...

Write anyway, even if it's on a different project, one that's not as important.

The problematic one will be right there waiting.

If you're exhausted and words seem like the enemy, write anyway.

It builds character. And confidence.

Write anyway, even if you're sure there's a worldwide conspiracy of corporations, government agencies, secret organizations, alien lizard people, magi and library reader's groups whose sole agenda consists of keeping your work from the eyes of the public at large.

Because if you don't, the bad guys

win.

Write anyway, even if you'll never be as good as Writer XYZ.

Writer XYZ is actually just a figurehead anyway. Her work is actually written by committee - a committee consisting of members of the top echelon of the conspiracy against you.

Write anyway, despite the occasional bad review. Haters gonna hate.

The next word just won't come? Write anyway.

And then write more.

IV.

This happened to me in college, in the midst of a novella I was working on as my final thesis for an advanced creative writing seminar. I still believed in writer's block at the time, and I was fully in its throes.

I complained to my friend - bitched, really - about how this particular scene I was trying to write was impossible. I was never going to get through it.

This friend - he's a computer programmer now, writes apps for a living, writes YA novels on the side; you haven't heard of him (yet) - just laughed and said, "Write it anyway. It's due. Screw the grade. Finish the damn thing. You need to pass the seminar even if your work is crap. A C is better than an F."

So I wrote it anyway.

It was miserable. My worst writing ever.

Sick to my stomach, groaning, I showed the story to my friend to help with last-minute edits before turning it in.

He read it twice.

"Where's this miserable scene?"

he asked. "It's a fine story, far as I can tell."

He might have caught a typo or two, but he had no big edits to suggest.

I'm not going to tell you which one it is, but that story's still out there for you to read. And people *do* read it on a fairly regular basis, and most who review it seem to like the story.

But no one has ever commented on that particular scene, positive, negative or otherwise.

And, yeah, I got an "A" in the seminar.

V.

I'm writing this while dead-dog tired, just to prove a point.

I might not edit it, just to prove a point.

I went to bed after 1 a.m. last night, got up before 6. Yesterday started at the same hour - saw the kids and wife out the door, wrote for two hours, worked full hours at my day job, then taught three evening and night classes, the last one ending at 9:45 p.m. with a 45-minute drive home and an hour of helping a daughter with math homework.

This morning a half-hour of napping on the couch before the day job looks awfully tempting.

The words are lackluster and dragging.

The coffee's not helping.

You don't have to tell me. I *know* this essay sucks. (Did I *really* think googling a synonym for "abomination" and cutting and pasting the heretofore unbeknownst to me words *"lusus naturea"* would impress *anyone?)*

I know *I* suck.

But I'm writing anyway.

VI.

Tomorrow, if not later today, I'll get back to the problematic fiction piece.

It will still probably be problematic, but I'll write it anyway.

And, if you read it once it's published, I'd bet you the price of the book and then some you won't be able to tell which section was giving me fits.

Maybe.

Journal Prompts

1. What are your biggest barriers to a solid day's work? How might you get around these barriers? Think of both "baby step" ways and "big change" possibilities.

2. Make a long list of things that bug you about a) writing, b) certain other authors - it's your journal, it's okay to be specific and name names! c) the current state of the writing marketplace.

3. Make a long list of the things you *like* about the items in #2.

4. Make a list of reasons of why you don't actually suck. Refer to this list during the times you do think you suck.

5. Journal in detail about your single best and worst writing experiences. What new things can you learn from them now, looking back?

6. Force yourself to write a long

journal entry when you are physically exhausted. The topic, grammar, punctuation, none of that matters. Just don't put the pen down until you have three full pages or more.

Story Prompts

1. Write a story where procrastination gets your protagonist into major trouble, maybe even jail or worse.

2. Write a story where supernatural forces of which your protagonist is initially unaware are keeping him/her from finishing a specific, seemingly mundane task. Why do these forces wish to stop him/her?

3. Write a story about someone who thinks they have made a major, irreversible mistake, but in the end it turns out to have been beneficial to someone in some important way.

4. Write a story about an artist who, unbeknownst to him/her really does have a huge conspiracy trying to keep their work from the masses.

5. Write a story about a writer for whom it is actually dangerous to finish any piece of writing.

6. Consider the Biblical character Job. Write a story of a Job-like writer - anything and everything that can go wrong for a writer happens to this character. Why? How does (s)he rise out of it (if (s)he does)?

David Bain

The Whisperers,
The Shower Fairy,
The Road Gods

Ninety-nine percent of the time I'm an advocate of the "butt in chair in front of keyboard" method of beating writer's block. Butt in chair with pen and paper works fine too. Even pencil.

I don't believe in writer's block. The next sentence is always there, waiting to be written, and if you've been at this writing thing for a while, you should have a number of projects you could turn to at any given point - some of them already half-written, some of them just in the mental warehouse in your head.

But I do believe in The Difficult Project. I do believe in Challenging Yourself. I even believe in The Project I'm Not Good Enough to

Write Yet. I tried to write my first novel three or four times before I was good enough to actually write it. But meanwhile I wrote reams of short stories and poems and short essays.

But let's say you've got nothing on deadline and you're Challenging Yourself with The Difficult Project - or, worse yet, let's say it *is* something you're writing on deadline, something for which someone is going to pay you - or maybe grade you on - and *that's* turning into The Difficult Project.

Paint, paint, everywhere, and you're in the corner.

In other essays, I've advocated writing about what you're writing about in order to break the block.

But, okay, there are just days when you're fed up and you don't want to *do* that.

You're sick of the whole thing.

You never want to see another computer screen or flashing cursor again!

Been there.

My advice then is to *walk away from it.*

Yup, walk away from that corner you've painted yourself into, muss up the paint job, track that sticky wetness all over the place, leave your shoe prints on the lawn and walk away.

I'm a big fan of sudoku puzzles and I've found the same thing with some of the most difficult of these. I'll look at every box and row and column and while I know the answer is probably right there in front of me, staring me in the face, I just can't see it. So I'll walk away. And when I come back, be it minutes or hours later, I usually find the key move that breaks the puzzle open for me within a minute or less. Same thing with writing. The story or essay or novel might certainly *look* impossible to finish when you're sitting there, staring at it, but some time away, minutes or hours or days, lets you see it afresh.

I don't recommend leaving it alone for days, however. Mostly because there's really no reason to. A couple hours at the very most is all that's necessary, usually only one or two, if that, should break the next scene or movement open for you.

When I'm in this situation where the screws have tightened on my mind, I'll go do one of three things to get loose. I'll exercise, take a shower or go for a drive. Sometimes I'll do all three before going back to the keyboard - but I *will* always go back to the keyboard, the sooner the better.

Exercising might mean taking a walk or a jog, doing some jumping jacks or just swinging my arms around, hopefully not at anybody. Exercise is a good idea for writers anyway - too much butt-in-chair time has been proven unhealthy and I know too many writers who have forgotten that their body has a musculoskeletal system that extends past their typing fingers and the flexing motion required to bring beer and Cheetos to their lips.

Exercise gets us out of the three-pound box inside our skulls and back onto the physical plane. It releases endorphins, and, if done at the gym or with a good workout tape, also allows us to ogle prime examples of the human body to which we might aspire.

This getting out of the cage of your skull is what it's all about. Your subconscious will continue working on the problem at hand, while your writer's palette will be wiped clean, ready for an array of new ideas.

Quite often, I'll find solutions while I'm trudging on the treadmill, my mind basically a blank. It's like the most benevolent of ghosts whispering something in my ear. Solutions to The Difficult Project frequently materialize out of nowhere while exercising.

Similarly, I'm convinced there's an invisible fairy who lives in the shower. If I don't manage to get anything out of the jogging session other than sweaty and tired and gross, ideas toward a solution are almost always splatted on my head by The Shower Fairy. The shower is like a private meditation chamber, but with all sorts of other pleasant sensations - warmth and pleasant odors and soft washcloths and towels - added. There's probably not a more perfect, more comfortable set-up for generating ideas and solutions.

Except maybe driving.

We often get "into the zone" while driving alone. It's a highly receptive, highly reflective, highly *open* state. We might have a destination in mind, but, here at the wheel, we're actually free to go anywhere. We are free, at a whim, to take that random turn, to take the road less traveled.

There are gods in the pavement who toss ideas up left and right to solitary drivers, I swear it. The gods who live in the dark macadam under our wheels have been collecting tales from the subconscious minds of every other driver on the road. Now they are telegraphing them up to you while you're in your zone, in your accessible state.

One caveat: It's important that you sit back down and do the work as soon as possible. The Whisperers, the Shower Fairy and The Road Gods aren't terribly focused. Too much reliance on them and your mind overflows with too many concepts, too many possible directions or projects. Feeling set adrift in a wide ocean of idea is almost as bad as having none at all. Butt in chair in front of typewriter is not only the best way to avoid writer's block in the first place, it's also the best way to thank and appease those minor deities of gym, bath and highway, should you have to call on them.

Journal Prompts

1. Write in detail about where one of your best story, poem or essay ideas came from.

2. Describe at length what it is like to be "in the zone." Get poetic about it. Fill a full page at the very least.

3. Make a list of projects you are (or would be) afraid to take on. What's keeping you from trying them? What needs to happen before you do?

4. Go for a long drive. Take extensive notes on small (and big) details you observe, especially things you've never noticed before along otherwise familiar routes. Try to list every idea that floats through your head.

5. Take a long walk. Either during the walk or directly after, take extensive notes on how the walk makes your body feel, your muscles,

your brain. As with #4, note any interesting things you see, any interesting ideas.

6. How does your walking experience differ from your driving experience? How does it differ from a more intense workout? How does it differ from your "Shower Fairy" experience?

Story Prompts

1. Write a story about a ghost whispering stories to a writer.

2. Write a story about The Shower Fairy. What does (s)he look like? What sort of dialogue does (s)he use? Does (s)he actually live in the shower or only visit from elsewhere?

3. Write a "Walter Mitty" sort of story about a person or writer with too many imaginative ideas running through their head.

4. Write a story about a supernatural encounter on the highway. Why is the supernatural entity (or entities) on (or maybe even in) the road?

5. Write a story involving two characters meeting, centered around some form of exercise. Are the characters both habitual exercisers? How do they change because of the exercise? How does the exercise

figure into the plot?

6. Write a story about a creature that traps ideas and hordes them away, keeping them from the world.

The Camera

Most fiction writers I know often see their story unfolding like a movie in their heads. When the scene is in full motion, writers simply take what's happening on that mind-screen and add the emotions and the five senses. It's the most fluid mode of writing - you're mostly just transcribing what's happening.

But then you get stuck, and the movie stops on the most recent frame.

For me it's sometimes literally a freeze frame, like someone literally hit the pause button.

I tend to "talk out" what happens next until the movie picks back up. That is, I tend to switch from a mostly visual mode to a mostly language-based, expository, rumin- ating mode until the visual mode again takes over - that visual mode certainly seems to be the preferred mode, both for writers and for readers.

***

Most of the time, it seems the writer's cinematographer, the person who decides the camera angles, the lighting, how close-up or far away from the subject of the scene we are, is on autopilot. If we need a close-up on the hero's magic ring, chances are our inner cameraman has already zoomed in. If we need to see the mountain vista as our heroine crests it with her rocket ship, our widescreen image is right there, utterly breathtaking.

I sometimes wonder if it was like this before the advent of cinema, but our innate storyteller tends to be pretty good, in general at positioning the camera.

But what about when we hit that writer's block freeze frame?

***

Have you ever watched one of those videos that starts with, say, a neutrino and expands until it's a proton and electron and then a hydrogen molecule, which then grows into a drop of water, which then expands into an ocean, our planet, our solar system, then our galaxy and beyond?

The same infinite width and breadth are available to us while writing.

We probably have no need to jump from quark to galactic cluster in our romance novel, but playing with the camera in our freeze-framed scene can be liberating if we're stuck. Do some extreme close-ups and see what appears. What's that on her shoe? Where did the scratch on her leather belt come from? Did we realize there's an unsightly blob in her otherwise immaculately applied mascara? We hadn't known she wore that particular charm on her bracelet…

We can also pan out. Slowly at first is usually best…

Say, who's this filthy kid passing her on the city street?

And what's that object twinkling on the sidewalk ten feet down?

What's in that shop window up ahead?

Let's pick up a little speed, pull even farther back, veer off to the side a little, maybe rise ever so slightly above the heads of the crowd...

What if that dog in the park across the street were to chase an errant Frisbee that lofted her way on the breeze that's sweeping in from over the lake?

The lake, where perhaps her true love, a character we hadn't dreamed up until this very instant, is currently sailing.

Back and back, landscape rushing by us now, though we can slow and speed up, rise and descend whenever we wish. What's happening the next town over, the next county over, the next state over, that might affect our heroine?

***

Our camera can pass through walls.

It is impervious to fire.

It can see in the dark.

It can slow down time.

It can speed ahead of a bullet to see its intended target.

It can run backwards and see what was happening in a specific space ten seconds, ten hours, ten years, ten millennia ago.

Same goes for the future.

Our camera doesn't flinch.

Our camera can smell the spring fog and taste the cold of the winter air; it can feel the pelting of the rain, can hear the smallest sound under the floorboards.

Our camera can sit behind someone's eyes, record their joy and pain, their thoughts and hopes and fears.

Our camera can enter dreams.

Our camera can see an illness before a doctor diagnoses it.

Our camera records things our characters forget.

Our camera finds any and all treasures, be they hidden, buried, sunken or secret.

***

Lighting.

What is the slant of light through the window?

Is it as dark in the interrogation room as it is in your character's soul?

Or perhaps the all-revealing, too-bright fluorescent lighting is forcing him to confess to the crime?

Look at the way your inner cinematographer has chosen to light your scene. Your shrink would tell you there's often a reason it's lit that way. Even if the only reason is "because that's the way it would be lit in real life," working in a subtle description of the lighting almost always "illuminates" a piece.

Just as the lighting can transform a scene in a movie, finding reasons behind and the words to describe the light in a scene you're writing can ... well, it can place the scene in a whole new light for you.

***

Slow motion and close-ups can

be great while writing action scenes.

Sex scenes too.

***

I'm not saying you should write a screenplay. Screenplays are an entirely different beast from straight fiction. (Ironically, there's a lot your camera can do in a piece of fiction that it can't do in a screenplay.)

***

And there are also, of course, times in most short stories or novels where the camera should be turned off completely - exposition is not always a bad thing.

There are good reasons "show, don't tell" is a core rule, but the better writers know there are times when it is essential to break it.

***

There is literally nowhere your inner camera can't go. If a scene is vexing you, take conscious control of the camera and see where it takes you. Freeze the frame frequently and look around. Sometimes the trick is to let the camera surprise you - but just as often, the trick is to see what is already there.

***

"There is only you and your camera. The limitations in your photography are in yourself." - Photojournalist Ernst Haas

Journal Prompts

1. Write about your place in the world, in the universe, what it means to be a speck on a cosmic scale and yet have be made up of endless nerves, neurons, molecules, etc. possessing a possibly infinite imagination.

2. Go to several different locations - maybe just in your house, or maybe over the course of a week - and describe the quality of light in detail.

3. Wherever you're sitting, describe your environs in great detail. Then keep doing it, expanding your view via your imagination in ever-expanding increments until your view is similar to a map.

4. Similar to #3, try the same thought experiment, but imagine you are simply walking (or eventually floating) in a single compass direction until you've gone much farther than

you ever have in reality. Describe the details in your journal as you go.

5. Take your mental camera somewhere a human could never possibly go. Describe the environs (and anything that's happening!) in detail.

6. Think of a favorite scene from your life. Slow the scene down until it plays second-by-second. Write about what's different in each one of these frames - don't forget sensations, emotions, etc.

Story Prompts

1. Write a story that involves events on the macrocosmic, microcosmic and "regular" human level.

2. Write a story about infinitesimally small, intelligent beings attacking your protagonist.

3. Write a story (perhaps Lovecraftian, perhaps not) from the point of view of a being larger than the earth itself. Make the entity even bigger than that, if you want.

4. Write a story about two people traveling toward each other across vast distances, moving ever closer and closer, for a final, fateful meeting. The reason for their meeting might be benign and romantic or dark and suspenseful. You decide.

5. Write a story which involves a photograph as evidence. What important evidence was beyond the

edges of the photo?

6. Write a story that takes place in a single second. Depend upon your mental camera to focus in and out and move all around and provide the significant, necessary details. Limit your use of flashbacks.

David Bain

Sorry, You're Not Stephen.
And You're Not James, Either.

I had a friend in college - call him
an emo kid, call him a hipster, call
him a Goth; he was, in turn, all these
things - who, while in his cups one
night, confided in me that he knew his
writing was going to be as important
as James Joyce's. He was earnest,
completely serious, and would
probably have made the same
statement while sober, except, well,
this was college and sobriety didn't
much figure into our encounters.

Yeah, anyway, I looked him up on
the internet a little while back. He's a
librarian now, fronts a Joy Division
tribute band. Nothing of note
published. I found two poems on
websites not worth mentioning. In an
email exchange he admitted to three
novels "in progress." Been working

on them for "several years now."

I can't come down on him too hard though. In college, my aspiration was to be the next Stephen King. The million-sellers, the mini-series, the movies, the awards.

A lot of young writers aspire to King. I knew another guy in college who once proclaimed, "I've read so much Stephen King, I think I'm starting to write like him."

Guy's an accountant now, still an alright guy. But he stopped writing with nothing published. Ever.

Me? Well, some have called me prolific - I certainly *wouldn't* say that about myself - and I guess I write Stephen King-ish stuff, mostly, but, yeah, I'll freely admit that right now I have *slightly* fewer fans than S.K. and file in a *slightly* lower tax bracket. I remain optimistic about the possibilities of both of those things changing, but if they don't, shrug, I'm okay. I've got books I can point to on the shelf. Some people seem to have enjoyed them. Other people can enjoy them after I'm gone.

Here's another story: When I edited a small, but nationally distributed poetry magazine for a community college I taught for, back when submissions still came via envelopes, I received a phone call from the college's main office saying a poet was there to see me. That's strange, I thought. Most of the poets we published were spread across the country and even overseas. Maybe someone we'd published was passing through and decided on a quick visit? Alas, no. It was a local poet from the small farming town near the college. Upon her arrival at my office, she shoved a folder of poems into my hand and bid me read. They were …

okay, I guess, if you liked forced rhymes and religious verse. Unfortunately, the lady was not only convinced I'd go run screaming down the hall with the revolutionary awesomeness of her work, she was sure her work was going to change the face of poetry itself - the world, in fact. In her own words, her work had "power" and "summed up the human experience." I did my best to reserve too harsh a judgment, advising her to buy a volume of *The Poet's Market* and begin submitting. I'm not sure if she actually did that, but she never submitted anything to my magazine and … well, I'm pretty sure that, even if you live in Centreville, Michigan, from whence she hailed, you've never heard of her.

There's a reason you haven't heard of my Emo Goth Hipster friend, my Stephen King write-alike friend and my mysterious Queen Apparant of Poetryland. They each set the bar far too high. James Joyce changed the face of literature and we've never seen the true equal of *Finnegan's Wake*, nor will we; it's truly a one-time work. King makes it all look oh-so-easy, but the truth is he seems to have an almost unfathomable connection to the popular subconscious combined with a style that might seem *aw shucks* and unconsidered, but is actually rather unique and highly crafted in its own way. And poetry, well, good luck. Shallow, low-life comedians and rock stars might get HBO specials and private jets, but even the current national poet laureate is little more than a blip on the radar of popular culture.

The truth is, aspiring to too much kills many a project, many a spirit, many a career.

A couple things might happen when you set the bar too high:

1. You never finish anything - or you give up because the work's "not good enough yet." If you hold your first novel up against the best book you've ever read, it's very likely you'll see it as falling short. And your first impulse might be to fix it. Endlessly. Until it's as good as *The Portrait of the Artist as a Young Man*. Please don't. Give it three passes. No more than five. (Okay, some writers do *twenty*. Fine. But they set a limit and quit.) The point is, *end it at some point!* Set a date if you have to, but, *writer please*, don't endlessly tinker with your first three "in progress" books. Focus on *one*. Finish *one*. The trick is to find the point where it's good enough and move on to the next thing. Learn these words: "Good enough. Time to move on." Treat writing as a learning process. A lifelong learning process, taking place over a plethora of manuscripts.

2. You give up because "the world won't listen." Maybe you've finished that novel and you actually deem it as good as the best thing you've ever read. But, alas, the publishing company you sent it to … does not. But then … neither do your friends. Even your family members just smile and nod politely whenever you mention your book. *But! But! But!* Your very *soul* is in that novel! Can't they *see* this.? The truth is, they likely can't. What's utterly important to you simply might not be important to the world. Also, consider this, especially if you're young - what's important to you one year might not be important to you the next. People change, and it can take a while to find the true themes of your work. Simply put: *If you're alive, you still have more to say.* Keep writing. The next book might be the one people actually "get."

3. You give up because of rejection. #2 often happens because, when you set the bar too high, it's easy to come off as, at best, pretentious. At worst … well, you don't wanna know what you come off as. You want to encompass the known universe or revolutionize a genre in your novel, your poem, your essay, but the rest of the world just sees big words and overblown ideas. Yes, Bono, Wagner and Dostoyevsky might have pulled it off, but too often those who set out to save or change the world by themselves come off as horribly bombastic or, worse, simply naive or pathetic. Also, *pssst!* The problem might just be *that you're* *simply not as good as you think you are; you need more practice.* It's important to note that this advice - let me repeat it: *you're simply not as good as you think you are; you need more practice* - can be good for writers and artists to consider throughout their career, not just at the beginning!

I think one of the most fortuitous quotes I ran into during my formative writing years is by horror writer Charles L. Grant, whom I wish was world-renown, but whom you probably haven't heard of if you're not a fan of horror paperbacks written from about the late 1970s to the early 2000s. Grant was a great literary stylist with a strong sense of imagery, lyricism, and a decided preference for subtle "quiet" horrors. Grant was always being compared to Stephen King. (Actually, *everybody* in horror was *always* being compared to King during those years.) Grant's response? "I'm not the new Stephen King, I'm the same old Charlie Grant."

Grant wasn't dissing King, not by any means. He was simply claiming ownership of his own work. Grant wasn't worried about having accolades and TV miniseries and movies - though he eventually garnered some awards and a small amount of Hollywood attention – he wrote some *X-Files* stuff, for instance. But, ultimately, he was worried about getting to the next story, and the next, and writing them well.

And I think that's the key. Even King has claimed that he writes first and foremost not for his editor or for what the market wants, but to please himself.

The best writers I know - and I'm talking about the best writers I know *personally*, not the best writers I know *of* - set bars for themselves that tend to be smaller, more personal in nature - maybe it's word count per day or a certain number of stories per year or to keep submitting to a certain magazine until they finally make it in. It's fine to aspire, to work, to strive, to aim for that icon in the sky, but in the end, great writers write because *that's what they do*.

Any success is gravy.

Journal Prompts

1. What is your definition of success in writing?

2. What traits of your favorite writer do you know you can emulate? Which do you have trouble with?

3. What started you on the road to writing? Why do you continue?

4. What is the best accolade you could receive?

5. What reaction to your writing has surprised you the most?

6. How have your outlooks on writing changed since you started? What - if anything - has stayed the same?

Story Prompts

1. Write a story about the most pretentious person possible.

2. Write a story about an artist or craftsman who never finishes their great project.

3. Write a story about a beginning artist who wakes up one morning to find they have switched places with the artist who first inspired them.

4. Write a story in the form of an acceptance speech which reveals more about the speaker than the speaker realizes.

5. Write a parody of a story, poem or essay by your favorite all-time writer.

6. Write a story about a person whom the world literally will not listen to.

David Bain

Sitting Cross-Legged
on the Kitchen Counter

I often ask my students where they write.

Most of them, of course, describe a desk in their house.

Bed seems a popular place, especially for those who write longhand or on a tablet or phone - laptops can be a little unwieldy in comparison.

The library, the coffee shoppe, the kitchen table, the couch, all are popular answers as well.

But one student caught my attention when he said, "I move every fifteen minutes. It keeps my perspective fresh."

I could identify. I myself have mild A.D.D. as a writer - an hour at the keyboard on the same project, two tops, and I'm pretty much spent on that project for the day. I can work harder on deadline; I can work on another project, but my attention span is short.

But to move locations every fifteen minutes?

"The kitchen, the couch, the bedroom, outside, pretty much every place anyone's mentioned, I spend a little time at each for almost every paper," the student continued.

I've long urged my students to practice writing in any situation - if you think you need quiet, go somewhere loud and try to write. If you normally write early in the morning, try squeezing in a few words at night - it's fine to write in your optimum setting, but it's useful to trust your voice in whatever situation you find yourself in when life gives you a few spare minutes.

But I'd never thought of this

musical chairs approach. I'd never thought of consciously and frequently moving during a single short-term project. My first thought was that you would *lose* focus, not gain it. You'd just be getting started, but then you'd have to get up and switcheroo again, off to a new location.

So I tried it a few times. What intrigued me is that, at least in my experience, you become more aware that *you are writing in a place.* That is, the document remained the same document, but when the location, the sounds, the chair beneath me, and so forth changed, it seemed to make me hyper-aware that I was *in control* of the piece.

Sitting in one spot with a difficult piece can feel like you're having an argument. You're grumbling back and forth with the document you're working on and you're not allowed to leave until the argument is over, until you and the piece of writing at hand have worked things out. "Don't go to bed mad," is common advice to newlyweds.

But taking the tough piece of writing to a new location is like grabbing the unruly child by the ear and walking them off around the corner where you're going to give them a *real* earful.

So while I still usually sit at my desk like everybody else, if looking at my Word file starts to feel more like a domestic dispute than a writing session, I'll take the laptop to the living room or dining room table or somewhere and, more often than not, the document starts seeing things my way after the change in locales.

And yet I still found myself thinking about the student's comment about keeping your perspective fresh.

It reminded me of a picture in Jill Krementz's wonderful book of photography, *The Writer's Desk*. The book is exactly what its title suggests, pages and pages of pictures of writers at their desks. Sounds thrilling, right? Actually, it kind of is, if you're a writer. All the writers in the book are famous, and each photo is accompanied by a blurb about the writer's process. But what's fascinating is the clear proof, evident there in the photographs, that there is no *right* way to do this writing thing. Every sort of desk is pictured - cluttered, tidy, cramped, open, makeshift, formal, tiny, huge, hi-tech, Luddite.

But then there's this wonderful picture of writer Veronica Chambers sitting cross-legged in a white dress on the kitchen counter of a small apartment, typing intensely away on her laptop. The picture appears merely charming at first, but in the blurb alongside the picture, Chambers discusses how she seeks high places in which to write so that she can metaphorically look out over her family's painful history and rule over what she surveys in order to find the proper perspective to finally write about it.

. Was Chambers simply posing, performing a silly stunt for the camera? My guess is not - she looks far too engrossed in whatever's on her screen for that. Now, for all I know, she could have been playing *Duke Nukem* or whatever other computer game was popular in 1996, the date on the photo, but, looking through the book, I'm surprised by how often you can draw a similar metaphor between author and the space in which they work.

The poets - John Ashberry, Nikki Giovanni - write in compact spaces. E.B. White, a champion of plain style, writes in an empty, austere cabin. Kurt Vonnegut and Stephen King have offices that could be kindly characterized as "lived in" if not downright disorganized, but both look wonderfully comfortable and at ease in such surroundings. John Irving's office is walled with broad windows that look out on expansive, lush scenery.

The late John Updike, who wrote the intro to the book, tells readers he has three offices. The first is for business correspondence and the accompanying photo shows a fax machine and other business accoutrements. Updike's fiction writing office is more like a library. And from what we can see from the angle from which it's shot, Updike's third office, existing solely for the writing of poetry - we should all be so lucky - contains a single window out which Updike can gaze, fist to chin, looking poetically contemplative.

So that's another thing that seems to help while writing a difficult passage - finding a space that's a metaphor for the way you want to write, allowing your surroundings, the space in which you write, to become a metaphor for what you want get down in words. Try writing by a river to make your sentences flow. Try writing in a plain and empty space if you want to simplify your language.

Most days, your routine office desk, as messy or clean as you like it, should do just fine. As long as we remember, as writers, that the space in which we're practicing our art can indeed make a difference at times.

Write Anyway!

Journal Prompts

1. Make a lengthy list of places you could conceivably go to write, but haven't yet. Now add places that might not be as easy to get to. Now add impossible places!

2. If you could have separate rooms for different specific types of writing, what would each look like? How would they differ? How might they be the same?

3. Consider a place from your past that has changed, perhaps drastically, perhaps only a little bit. Describe the different eras in detail. Describe events, observations and your emotions in both eras.

4. What would be the most uncomfortable writing situation possible for you? Describe it in great, excruciating detail.

5. Especially if you've never seen what their writing space looks like, describe the writing desk and room or other writing area, as you imagine it, for your favorite writer.

6. Pay close attention the next time a movie or TV show you're watching portrays a writer or artist at work. What do they get right? Do they get anything noticeably wrong? What can you take away from this. Perhaps expand this to the portrayed writer's entire lifestyle.

Story Prompts

1. Write a story with at least three wildly different locations. Make each of the locations necessary to the story.

2. Your protagonist wakes up in an unusual spot (perhaps just once, perhaps many times). (S)he does not have a history of sleep-walking…

3. Your protagonist consciously decides upon a drastic shift in living quarters. Why? (Hiding out is a perfectly acceptable but relatively easy reason. What might be funny, romantic, scifi or fantasy reasons? What's a serious mainstream literary reason?) Make sure the old and new environs are essential to the plot.

4. Write a character with a severe physical ailment, where their body cannot go where most people can go. Handicapped, ill or otherwise impaired characters – how does their limited range of motion and location affect the story?

5. Have a character revisit a special place that changes. Maybe it

changes once, maybe it changes several times throughout the story.

6. Write a story about a place a human couldn't go – at least not for long: underwater, outer space, inside a volcano, under a polar ice cap.

Dancing in Your Chair

Sometimes I will write at the kitchen table while my family does other things around me. If it's going well, I get lost in the words and don't even pay attention to the outside noise and activity. That's mostly likely when my family will accuse me of "dancing in my chair."

It's a technique I use to keep the writing fresh, unique and specific.

Whenever there's an action or motion in the scene I'm writing, I often tend to make an associated gesture. I might punch the air, kick or dodge a blow if I'm writing a fight scene. I rarely get up to actually act out the scene with my full body, but I will gesticulate, sometimes fairly wildly, my hands and arms becoming substitutes for the brawlers' bodies.

There's a reason the best storytellers - and arguers and even political speakers - gesticulate a great deal when they are practicing their craft in front of a crowd. The gesticulations, though they're usually little more than subtle hand gestures, help the audience to "see" the scene that's being told or the point that's being discussed. The gesture helps the viewer's imagination to fill in that much more of what the speaker is asking them to picture.

Similarly, when you as a writer find yourself temporarily stuck, staring at the screen, knowing generally what you want to say but not exactly how to say it, taking your hands off the keyboard and working it out through gestures can be immensely helpful. Before long, the words your brain is trying to find slip into place, your hands descend back to the keys, and you're off and typing again. (II usually find this technique facilitates word count per unit of time rather than the time with your fingers off the keys being a detriment - I usually don't have to gesticulate for very long at all.)

This also helps a lot with dialogue. Make the gestures your character would make while speaking his or her lines. You'll end up with more reader-engaging motion following the quotation marks and less repetitive, glossed over he-saids and she-saids.

And while I certainly use this technique a lot to discover and add descriptions and details about my characters' motions, there's much, much more you can do with it.

Just in the last 48 hours, I've used hand motions and gesticulations to help myself discover words for –
    * the quality of light in a room
    * how it would feel to fly
    * the gentleness of the rain
    * the density of the fog
    * how fast a car took off
    * how a character's loneliness feels

It seems strange to me that the gestures and the words that wind up on the page are often at least seemingly unrelated. Yes, for the rain

I made rain gestures with my fingertips and the car took off like a slashing hand between myself and the computer screen. It might even be somewhat predictable that my character's loneliness feels like a fist clenching and re-clenching tighter and tighter near the solar plexus and heart. But for the flying I made motions more akin to a mime pretending to be stuck in a box, which doesn't at all mirror the words that came to mind and ended up on the page. And I found the words for the fog by what might look like I was wadding up a huge ball of invisible paper - which is certainly not what even dense fog feels like. And no soft sunlight ever flailed around like my hands did when finding the words for a curtained room.

The point here is to just let the gesture happen - no one's grading you on its appropriateness. No one but you is taking notes.

Perhaps the strangest "dancing in my chair" I do happens when I'm not exactly sure what comes next. I might have a general idea in the form of an outline, if I happen to be using one, but the phrasing or segue isn't quite there yet, hasn't quite gelled.

I'll sit there, staring intensely at the screen, as if I'm fully engaged in … I don't know. An intense conversation? An argument? A staring contest? Doesn't matter. But I'll start making gestures like I'm talking to it. I'll let my fingers and hands zig and zag, point or bounce. My hand might flop around, ball up, give a high-five. I might caress or snatch or knock over something that isn't there. Sometimes there's a rhythm to the gesticulation, like I'm a rapper spitting his rhymes with a breathtaking flow, though I'm not actually moving my lips and I'm hearing no verbiage at all. Sometimes I feel like I'm the director of a play or movie, giving directions for arranging a set or blocking a scene. The gestures, to my conscious mind, at least, are completely meaningless, but I have a feeling they're getting the worker bees in my subconscious riled up, searching for words to accompany them.

I firmly believe that, even if you're doing this in a public place, you have to be unashamed of the gestures - it's what garners the best words. If someone looks at you funny or asks what you're doing, just explain to them - these days my family just laughs and keeps on walking by, but, hey, if it's a stranger, their question can be a great lead-in to the fact that you're a writer and they should buy your books!

Finally, I also recommend gesticulating as you re-read your work while editing. Again, when I'm looking over my own work after a first draft, I'll often look like a rapper, delivering words to the beat. I'm definitely not saying you should be writing your words in iambic pentameter or to any specific beat, but gesturing while you read will help you feel if the words are flowing and if your reader is going to cruise through them at the pace you want them to. If your gesticulating hand hesitates or seems to "hiccup" as you're going through your draft, you might want to reconsider the wording of that particular phrase or passage.

Journal Prompts

1. Try to describe the "shape" of a particular sound. Set your pen down, use your hands – perhaps while actually making the sound. Do the same for a concept or physical things listed above – rain, fog, etc.

2. Everyone has some habitual, almost unconscious motions – tapping fingers, rubbing a beard, etc. Observe the people around you for a day, taking notes.

3. Describe in detail all the particular body motions you yourself do when you dance to a rock and roll song. How about the other dancers around you?

4. Watch a video of someone doing tai chi. Describe the motions in detail. Try to keep your word choice varied.

5. Sports writing and sports announcing can be harder than they

look. Describe in detail the motions on the field and the motions of particular athletes.

6. Make a long list of the sounds around you that you usually don't notice as you go about your day.

Story Prompts

1. Research how different seemingly mundane motions are interpreted around the world – for instance, using the "come over here" forefinger gesture in the Philippines can actually get you arrested! Write a related story.

2. Similar to #1, write a story about an innocent gesture that's totally misinterpreted and causes anything from a humorous to fatal misunderstanding. This could take place in anything from out mundane mainstream world to a far-out fantasy or scifi setting.

3. Write about a character who, due to physical or other limitations, does not have a normal range of motion. Put them in jeopardy.

4. Write about a character who is totally unashamed about what (s)he does/says/thinks, etc. Write about a

character who thinks *too much* about every last little thing they think, do or say.

5. Write about a person who is directing a play or a movie, but the action starts taking off far beyond his/her control.

6. A writer is taken over by the actions of his or her character, perhaps only while sitting at the keyboard, perhaps in the world at large…

Write Anyway!

Genre-Jump Your Story

One of the more interesting techniques I've found for getting your story unstuck is to write the next scene as if you'd been working in a totally different genre all along.

While I tend to be very much against the over-categorization and pigeonholing of fiction in general - and especially mine - there's little or no denying that certain genres of fiction have over-the-top tropes and icons and, yes, even cliches.

When you're stuck or unmotivated about the next scene you have to write - or perhaps it's even the next complete story or novel you're procrastinating about - doing a sketch of it in a genre completely unrelated to the one you envision for it can sometimes break things wide open for you - especially if you write it in over-the-top cliched genre stereotypes.

Here is an example from my own experience.

In my first novel, *Gray Lake*, which the subtitle handily refers to as a novel of crime and supernatural horror, I needed to figure out how Mike Menger - an anti-hero, somewhat antagonistic figure - first met his true love Rosie. Both of their pasts are shrouded in secrecy, so I couldn't go back too far, and neither of these characters is particularly, shall we say, genteel. They are brash, outspoken and unrefined. So how do characters like that get together.

I was at a complete loss.

Until I imagined them as ogres.

I realized that, were their story to be set in a fairy tale world, Mike would simply be a very intelligent ogre, and Rosie is his ogre princess - maybe like Princess Fiona in *Shrek*.

At first I just found this parallel amusing. But then I started thinking about how Menger would rampage through faery kingdoms and so forth, and I started to wonder how he might wind up with his ogrish bride. I certainly couldn't call on any more parallels to *Shrek* because, if you've read the book, Menger is most likely not going to rescuing a princess from a lonely, heavily booby-trapped castle.

Actually, he might, but he'd curse the entire way and, once he was done, he would give the princess the finger and tell her to shut up and never tell anyone about it lest it ruin his reputation as a scary badass.

No, what Menger would do in the distorted fairy tale I was imagining was *kick the crap out of another ogre,* probably one two times his own size, laughing maniacally as he did so, stealing the princess away as his rightful prize and she'd be the type of princess who'd damned well be happy about it - Menger's not much of a women's libber, either.

I actually wrote the scene in full fairy tale mode in a journal somewhere. It's pretty funny - at least I thought so. The earth is shaken with bodyslammed ogre butts. Peasant huts are crushed. There's a lot of over-the-top smack-grunting and over-the-head clubbing and gnashing and smashing of big, pointy teeth.

It broke the scene I had to write for *Gray Lake* wide open for me. I simply had to translate my fractured fairy tale fight scene into my contemporary setting. But either way the scene still breaks down to two ogres fighting over a princess who's barely better-looking than either of the brawlers.

This exercise affected the way I looked at the rest of *Gray Lake* and a lot of my subsequent fiction. I realized, for instance - and I have a character realize as much in a passage toward the end of the book - that in different stories told in different settings or eras, the supernatural dreamlike Queen figure who enters the town of Green River in a haunted car would be a witch flying in from the dark woods on her broomstick or perhaps a dragon cruising in from the blasted lands on the foul nightwind.

Even most straight-up literary mainstream fiction deals in archetypes. Sure we might play with archetypes, try to subvert or reroute or challenge or deny what they stand for, but that doesn't change that the archetype is there in the first place.

Thinking about or writing about your characters as if they had stepped into a different genre gives you insight as to who your character really is, what they're all about, and what's at their core. It shows you how they are *in their essence*.

While this tactic can be a breakthrough for entire scenes, it can also be a boon to your character's dialogue. I'm not saying the inner city kid who you've just imagined as a knight-in-training should start speaking in thees and thous, but he might indeed start subtly taking on a more literate, self-assured verbiage in certain situations when he knows he's in the right. Similarly, it might have helped you to freewrite the next scene with your archeologist professor turning into a hard-boiled, fedora-wearing detective, but he can go back to wearing his pith helmet and speaking softly in multi-syllabic words as he always has - except maybe with a little more bite in this particular scene. What's important is that you found this hard-boiled undercurrent to his otherwise contemplative, academic persona, an undercurrent that might serve to aid him in getting through yet-to-be-written scenes as well.

I don't think anyone but me has likely pictured ogres when reading the scene where Menger wins Rosie in a raucous brawl. Similarly, no one needs to know that, for a difficult scene or two, you pictured the dad in your quiet mainstream novel as a star fleet captain, or that your unicorn-riding scullery maid-turned-warrior-princess was, for a short while, a high powered Manhattan corporate lawyer, having risen up from the ranks of the secretarial temp pool.

Even if you are not a writer of genre fiction, even if you wouldn't be caught dead allowing your name on a horror, fantasy, romance, science fiction or Western novel, we all have a little bit of gunslinger, a little bit of hobbit, a little bit of ghoul and a little bit of romantic waif in us - and so does your character. Let them express it from time to time, and let it expand your fiction!

Journal Prompts

1. What is a genre you would "never touch" as a writer? Explain in detail the reasons you'd never go there.

2. Take a look at your journaling from prompt #1. Make a list or otherwise brainstorm about what changes you could make to the genre's tropes so you would find writing in it more acceptable.

3. Write a scene in your favorite author's voice, but change the author's usual genre.

4. Make a list of familiar, popular and your favorite books. Now, next to that list, make several columns. Label each column with a different genre – horror, science fiction, romance, etc. – and give each book an alternate title for each genre. That is, think like a marketer – how would a book marketer change the title if the same

story idea were written for a different genre? The title can be similar to the original, but doesn't have to be.

5. Take one of your favorite memories – or maybe one of your worst memories – and write a detailed recollection, but as if it were a genre story. Be over the top with the genre tropes and writing style.

6. Examine your writing space or another specific, fairly ordinary setting. Write a solid paragraph describing it. Now rewrite the paragraph in a different genre. And another different genre.

Story Prompts

1. Write a story about a character whose world exists firmly in one genre who must adjust to life in a totally different genre.

2. Write a story about a character whose world exists firmly in one genre who encounters and must deal with an object from a totally different genre.

3. Write a story in which your genre characters perform a story from another genre – for example, write a romance whose main characters happen to be superheroes – there's no supervillain or world-wide danger to overcome; there's just a romance story.

4. If you have a Netflix account, go to your main page and write down the genre titles above the many lists provided there for you. Combine three of those genres and write a story. (If

you don't have a Netflix account, make a long list of very specific genres (i.e. Victorian ghost stories, international conspiracy thriller, dark science fiction anime, etc.) and combine three genres at random.

5. Steal and rewrite a classic story. Many, many popular stories and novels, genre and otherwise, are loosely based on mythology or children's stories or Shakespeare, for instance. Do your own "borrowed" story.

6. Try a mash-up. There have been several bestsellers along the lines of *Pride and Prejudice and Zombies.* Try your own. (Public domain works are safest for this and prompt #5 in terms of copyright.)

Join the WRITE THOUGHTS newsletter for monthly tips, news, author interviews & more!

You get a free ebook just for signing up - WRITE BECAUSE! featuring more journal ideas, story prompts and essays that *obliterate* writer's block!

http://smarturl.it/WriteThoughts

Word-of-mouth is crucial for any author to succeed. If you enjoyed this story, please consider leaving a review on Amazon or on Goodreads, even if it's only a line or two; it would make all the difference and would be very much appreciated!

Connect with David Bain

Newsletter: http://smarturl.it/FriendsOfBain
(You get two free novellas just for signing up!)
Website: http://DavidBainBooks.com
On Kindle: http://smarturl.it/DavidBainKindle
On Audible: http://smarturl.it/DavidBainAudible
Twitter: http://twitter.com/davidbainaa
Facebook:
https://www.facebook.com/david.bain.16
Pinterest: http://pinterest.com/davidbainaa
Rebel Mouse:
http://RebelMouse.com/davidbainaa
Goodreads: http://bit.ly/DavidBainGoodreads

Visit Beautiful Green River, Michigan!
http://bit.ly/GreenRiverMichigan

CPSIA information can be obtained
at www.ICGtesting.com
Printed in the USA
LVOW13s1910060517
533526LV00002B/69/P